EMPOWERING ARCHITECTURE
Butaro Hospital, Rwanda

STRATEGIES TO IMPROVE HEALTH AND
STRENGTHEN COMMUNITY THROUGH
ARCHITECTURE AND DESIGN

By MASS Design Group
Photos by Iwan Baan
and MASS Design Group

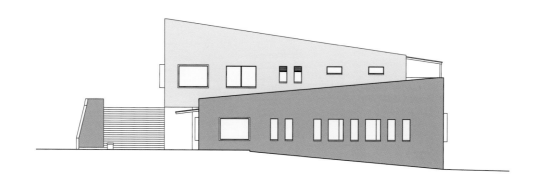

EMPOWERING ARCHITECTURE

CONTENTS

UGANDA

DEMOCRATIC
REPUBLIC OF THE
CONGO

BUTARO

BURERA
DISTRICT

TANZANIA

KIGALI

RWANDA

BURUNDI

RWANDA REBUILT
Paul Farmer, MD PHD

Dr. Paul Farmer talks with Rwandan President Paul Kigame at the Butaro Hospital inauguration.

A hospital is never intended as a metaphor—the work that goes on within is, or should be, far more literally life-saving—but the Butaro Hospital serves as a potent symbol of rebirth. The word "Rwanda" carries, for most non-Rwandans, images of mass violence and not of verdant, volcanic mountains. That should begin to change. A mere 16 years after the genocide, a former Rwandan military base on the Ugandan border has been reborn as one of the loveliest hospitals on the continent, as even the briefest visit—or these stunning photographs by Iwan Baan—will attest.

My 25 years of practicing medicine in some of the poorest places in the world have taken me through hundreds of clinics and hospitals in 20 or more countries. Some of the most discouraging moments in medical work occur because these facilities are poorly designed or poorly stocked or dirty. Not only are the wretched of the earth forced to endure high risk of premature death (and high probability of unnecessary suffering), they have to do so in dismal conditions—in clinics that are unclean, unlovely, and staffed, if they are staffed at all, by poorly trained and overworked providers. Grim, dank and sometimes deadly, these facilities constitute their glancing contact, if ever they have one, with modern biomedicine. Such contact is the opposite of true hospitality.

Public-health authorities in the poor world, or international health NGOs, must wage many battles at once: among them, the battle to build and equip hospitals and clinics and the battle to keep them clean, staffed and stocked. But doctors and nurses are not typically trained to design and build hospitals. In the case of Partners In Health, this work fell into our hands because we had in our network too few health professionals fighting for the destitute sick—the very patients who ought to be medicine's primary concern—and even fewer professionals from the world of building construction and design. It is true that a welcoming, modern mission hospital may be built from time to time in rural Africa, but rare indeed are *public* facilities on that continent that show the mark of those trained to design and bring into being beautiful and safe buildings. It's as if the science of design had missed entirely the people who might most benefit from it.

As interest in global health grows, as sharp and longstanding divides between rich and poor are at last revealed, as new communication platforms make distances shrink, more and more expert attention is turned to long-neglected social problems and challenges, including health equity. The Butaro Hospital, a public facility, draws on this emerging field and on expert mercy; it draws on the capable and resolute optimism of Rwandan leadership, local and national. The building gives a physical locus to the unprecedented surge in the expert attention of Rwandan (and other) medical professionals to the unmet needs of the people of rural Rwanda.

This hospital is thus also a metaphor for the partnerships that were always intended to constitute Partners In Health. Many private donors, the Nova family chief among them, contributed to the Butaro effort. So did the Clinton Foundation: President Clinton and his daughter Chelsea broke the ground on top of the mountain in August 2008. But in the construction of any public facility, one of the chief partners in question is invariably the public sector, which is charged with assuring the health of the population. The Republic of Rwanda has been the best of all partners: heavily engaged in every step of the way and assuming responsibility for Butaro Hospital's maintenance and management. (Rwanda does this nationwide, devoting more than 10% of its public budget to health care, more than most other countries in the region; it is on track to meet pledges made to reach more than 15%.)

Public-sector engagement starts at the level of the town, Butaro; moves on to the district, Burera; and the Northern province, and then to the nation. Officials from each of these levels of government were involved in the Butaro effort, which helped create thousands of jobs in the short time it took to build the hospital. Job creation is valuable in the long run only if the structures built are worthy of the labor: surely the pyramids of Giza consumed the labor of thousands, too, but left them no richer than before. The people of Burera district knew that their labors were an investment in an effort to promote broader efforts to link village health workers to clinics and then to a hospital, the first in a region that, as recently as 2004, could not boast a single physician—much less a hospital. Now more than a dozen physicians and three-score nurses staff the hospital. In addition to the wards you can see in these photographs, it boasts digital radiology and an electronic medical record system.

A beautiful built environment might not be as essential to healing as a clean one, but there is no reason to choose beauty over cleanliness or efficiency or innovation. And how better to incorporate respect for our patients and their families than to focus on dignity and design? In 2005, during our first year in Rwanda, we had a visit from a colleague and friend from Mexico. Julio Frenk had been Mexico's Minister of Health, and while in office launched some of the world's most ambitious efforts to link provision of health services to poverty reduction by protecting tens of millions of citizens from the threat of impoverishment due to catastrophic or chronic illness. Dr. Frenk, now the dean of the Harvard School of Public Health, visited rural southeastern Rwanda as some of us were putting the finishing touches on a koi pond in the middle of the grounds of another public hospital, in the town of Rwinkwavu. Dr. Frenk understood our purpose right away. He might have been surprised to find his medical colleagues working after hours to spruce up the grounds just as assiduously as they'd rebuilt and stocked the hospital and its clinics; but did not hector us about "unnecessary expenditures." Nor had our partners from the Rwandan government: Rwinkwavu Hospital, which had been abandoned

after the war and genocide, is now surrounded by gardens which are the first thing visitors comment upon. They cost just a few thousand dollars to design and plant, and their effect on morale is significant. Frenk looked around the grounds of a previously desolate hospital and termed what we were doing *dignificacíon*: Spanish for rendering dignified.

How is it that the most mediocre tourist hotels in the world's cities are still better and cleaner than the best rural hospitals in Africa and much of Latin America? Partners In Health has come a long way from its humble beginnings in rural Haiti, and we are now running 70 health facilities serving almost exclusively the poor. The Butaro Hospital moves our collective dream of *dignificacíon* forward. The campus is laid out around courtyards, with the way marked by placards designed by graphic designer Massimo Vignelli and team. The signage, in English and Kinyarwanda, is color-coded for those who cannot read. In addition to gardens with fish ponds, the outdoor areas include generous porches where patients can sit and talk as they convalesce. And although it's a steep mountaintop campus, ramping makes the hospital wheelchair-accessible.

Dignificacíon is in evidence, we hope, in the wards, in the hand-hewn volcanic-rock walls, in the signage, and also in the gardens. This is in part thanks to landscape architect Sierra Bainbridge, a former project manager of the High Line, which took an old elevated freight line cutting through the heart of New York City and turned it into a stunning public space. Bainbridge and others—I was proud to be among them—built the Butaro gardens with local flora. These restful grounds are watched over by a massive ficus tree, an *umuvumu* that, according to Rwandan tradition, once marked the places where the king and his court lived or camped. Our patients deserve nothing less: Butaro's *umuvumu* towers over the peaceful courtyard as a symbol of the reverence we feel for our patients and their families. They are, we hope, the kings in our kingdoms, the people for whom we erect palaces of healing and repose.

Beautiful design does not, however, lead to good health unless it makes hospitals *effective* and *safe*. Risks from what our architect colleague Alan Ricks terms the "poorly built environment" include falls, injuries, and nosocomial infections. Across the world, hospitals can be deathtraps. Airborne infections, especially tuberculosis, are too commonly acquired during hospital stays or clinic visits. Studies from South Africa and elsewhere suggest that, among people living with AIDS, the chief risk factor for dying from drug-resistant tuberculosis has been showing up to clinic—following doctors' orders.

The Butaro Hospital draws on strategies for *beautiful* hospital design, but it's our hope that it serves as a how-to example for *better* hospital design. For example, improving ventilation through the design of redundant systems to lessen risk of airborne infection: improved circulation of exterior air; a mix

ultraviolet lights (at our suggestion, MASS co-founder Michael Murphy took the time to take a class at Harvard called "Engineering methods to control airborne infections"). Every bed faces a beautiful view, whether of the courtyard gardens or the surrounding valleys. In all respects, the design is patient-centered and functional.

The architecture here responds to real problems, and does so in creative and efficient ways. Why are there so few examples of this kind of thoughtful, generous-spirited design? The most honest answer to this question turns on the "political economy" of design: those who have the resources determine who will design what, when, and where. Further issues have to do with implementation: even when a facility is designed to serve the public without restrictions, the users' needs are assumed to be known in advance. One of the unusual strengths of Butaro Hospital is that it made the unusual leap from concept to construction through an exchange that pushed designers and engineers to listen to us, the health care providers; and, with us, to our patients.

The MASS architects and designers came to live with us up in Butaro. They listened to our complaints and our concerns; they listened to Rwandan engineers and builders, including Bruce Nizeye and his construction team. They engaged in what they called immersive research (every field has it; anthropologists call it field work and doctors call it

I believe that this experience—the progress from design to implementation through listening – is reflected in this book's three sections: user experience, contextual response, and community impact. These headings translate readily into obvious and important categories for any doctor or nurse who seeks to improve public health.

It's a relief to have a global health equity team complemented by architects and engineers, in addition to the builders to whom we've had greater access. We're also so grateful for this book. I would like to thank the photographer, Iwan Baan, and the MASS architects and engineers, especially Michael Murphy, for their expertise, commitment, and optimism. We all need expertise, and often. But we also need ideas for change. As a physician and teacher, I am grateful to Michael for listening with attention when I spoke, in one of many talks that year to the broader Harvard community, about the need to bring all of our expertise to bear on the health problems of the world's poor. This included the need for "social-justice architecture," I said. But no phrase, however well-meant and sincere, could have brought about the founding of MASS; only architects and engineers could do that and did. Michael took up my challenge and kept his promises.

This community of designers cannot be limited to American designers. It must also include our peers and future peers in Africa, including the land of a thousand hills and ten times as many dreams. This hospital was built by Rwandans for Rwandans.

Beyond designing Butaro Hospital, the MASS team has helped to train young Rwandans to aim high. Sierra Bainbridge came to teach the next generation by helping to create, under the leadership of the Rwandan Ministry of Education, the country's first school of architecture and environmental design. It is Partners In Health's hope that all of our projects lead to similar training programs, programs nourished by the lessons learned in the course of delivering health services. The country's first class of architects, 25 strong, will graduate soon. We have so much work to do, and will need to draw on their imagination and vitality.

Finally, I would like to thank those who helped to create a health system linking Butaro Hospital to health centers, towns, and villages: Minister Agnes Binagwaho, Governor Bosenibamwe Aimé, Mayor Sembagare Samuel, Dr. Tharcisse Mpunga, Didi Bertrand Farmer, Dr. Michael Rich, and Dr. Peter Drobac. President Paul Kagame, who cut the ribbon of Butaro Hospital in January, has been an unstinting supporter of our work.

Failures of imagination have doomed countless many to early suffering and premature death. Mediocre architecture and design have contributed to those failures, as have mediocre (or worse) governance and medicine and public health. Rwanda has been down that road before, and now rejects it, as we all should do. Let the Butaro Hospital serve as more than a metaphor. This hospital, as handsome as it is, does not fulfill its function by being taken as a model but as the "least common denominator," the least we can do to make manifest our respect for the poor and our commitment to building a genuine movement for global health equity. The next hospitals built in the service of the poor need to eclipse Butaro in every one of its admirable aspects. That's what global health equity means.

20 October 2011

THE WELL-BUILT ENVIRONMENT
Alan Ricks

THE POORLY BUILT ENVIRONMENT
Poorly built health infrastructure caused havoc in a rural region of South Africa in 2005. The lack of design and planning of the Tugela Ferry clinic led to overcrowding in poorly ventilated areas, ultimately resulting in the transmission of a fatal disease known as Extremely Drug Resistant Tuberculosis (XDRTB), which killed all 53 people infected. This incident shines a light on the role of the built environment and its effects on health outcomes—in this case in a profoundly negative and deadly way.

Poorly built environments, those that do not incorporate contextual needs, cripple the efforts of governments and NGOs aiming to provide necessary public services. Additionally, interventions often occur in isolation and focus on addressing immediate needs, failing to address the systemic changes necessary for long-term, sustained improvement.

The importation of foreign models of development, construction, and design processes often produce inappropriate solutions that fail to address their goals or are unsustainable over time. Architecture and design thinking processes are uniquely capable of providing both immediate and long-term planning to address issues at the scale of the discrete building, as well as the larger systems that impact the delivery of services.

THE WELL-BUILT ENVIRONMENT
Well-Built Environments, those that are efficient, effective, and empowering, result from architectural

thinking applied to the full project delivery process and engender social and political effects that help fight inequity. MASS Design Group was founded in order to understand and deliver projects based upon these principles.

This means addressing more than just a building's ventilation; it requires taking into account the training of health care workers to understand infection control strategies, the design of triage and patient flow, and the advocacy to improve health care delivery. This holistic approach to appropriate infrastructure is built upon extensive research and immersion on the ground. The underlying notion is that there is no silver bullet, no universal prototype, but rather a need to ask the right questions and patiently understand the unique requirements of each project and each community.

A PROCESS, NOT A PROTOTYPE

This book began as an effort to provide strategies for how to build better health infrastructure. What became increasingly evident, however, was that the contextual issues that each strategy must consider to be effective would vary. This book is a model of process rather than of product. Using the case of the Butaro Hospital, it examines how the holistic approach to creating Well-Built Environments delivers better services, positively impacts the community, and ultimately assists in breaking the cycle of poverty.

Applying design and architectural thinking to social justice goals can produce equitable infrastructure and assist our partners in addressing both short and long-term needs. The building itself serves as the platform for the delivery of better patient-centric services and dignity construction that responds to contextual issues. The building process is leveraged for community impact; serving as an engine of education, training, and job creation that reverberates far beyond the structure itself.

Told with the assistance of Iwan Baan's brilliant photographs, this book is a testament to a community that sought to rethink the role of infrastructure in serving its citizens, and the partners that signed on to make that a reality.

AN ARCHITECTURE OF SOCIAL JUSTICE
Michael Murphy

Quality architecture can no longer be determined by a photograph alone. Instead, buildings must be considered in terms of how society uses them over time with social and political implications governing success. Quality must be reframed to account for both the immediate and the long-term (socio-political) implications on the built environment.

Our work with Partners In Health (PIH) in Rwanda tells us that there are precedents for this type of analysis in medicine. For example, "distal" interventions are those performed in the late stages of illness, when patients are already sick. These approaches are immediate. The distal interventions stop the bleeding.

Proximal interventions, however, are those that address causes of disease. More than mere prevention, like providing water or vaccinations, proximal interventions look for the bio-social determinants of disease. Tuberculosis (TB), although curable and nearly eradicated in the US and Europe, kills thousands of people a day in developing economies. "It is a disease of poverty," PIH tells us, and proximal interventions address the structural conditions that allow people to develop TB – those that, not coincidentally, also keep people living in poverty.

Lack of access among the poor to health care, proper nutrition, and even housing are structural conditions that have direct outcomes on the virulence of a disease like TB as well as on mortality rates of a given population. Public health has developed much more comprehensive ways to both respond to these proximal conditions and quantify the cost, not only in dollars spent but also in lives lost, of failing to provide proximal interventions. The founder of PIH, Dr. Paul Farmer, tells us:

The debate about whether to focus on proximal versus distal interventions, or similar debates about how best to use scarce resources, is as old as medicine itself. But there is little compelling evidence that we must make such either/or choices: distal and proximal interventions are complementary, not competing.[1]

With architecture too, a narrowed frame that focuses only on the form of buildings produces a limited understanding of our built environment and thus a limited ability to change it. A narrowed frame restricts both the form the building can take (what we might call the distal considerations) as well as the processes that design, construct, and evaluate the building's impact over time (these are all proximal considerations).

As architects we lack precedents of what it would cost to not apply our training to a problem. Working on the Butaro Hospital has provided us the opportunity to quantify the value of design and revealed its impacts on the ability of communities to survive, and remain healthy. Architecture is an important proximal consideration of health. Architecture is also, as Dr. Zeynep Celik reminds

us, a crystallization of "social relations and power structures into form."[2]

Health care, too, is a crystallization of power into social relations, and in PIH's work, this means framing health care not only as access to medicine, but also as access to sanitation, access to employment, and even access to housing. These conditions affect people's health, and therefore are part of the doctor's purview.

Farmer characterizes these systemic failures as "structural violence," a way of describing social arrangements that put individuals and populations in harm's way. They are "structural," he tells us, "because they are embedded in the political and economic organization of our social world; they are violent because they cause injury to people." He continues:

Structural violence... describes social structures—economic, political, legal, religious, and cultural—that stop individuals, groups, and societies from reaching their full potential. In its general usage, the word violence often conveys a physical image; however, according to [Joseph] Galtung, it is the "avoidable impairment of fundamental human needs or...the impairment of human life, which lowers the actual degree to which someone is able to meet their needs below that which would otherwise be possible."[3]

Why can't architecture take a similar stance? What keeps architecture from measuring its ability to provide or prevent access to core services such as health care, education and employment? Certainly architects, by their deep relationships to power, affect these conditions. Why would Partners In Health spend their limited resources on housing and first-rate hospitals unless they considered them essential? The reverse is true as well. If the architectural paradigm is better-designed hospitals, then the success of a given project is measured by the socio-economic condition of the people that inhabit it. The individual's health, and her access to education and employment, will remain metrics of the building's success. What Farmer calls bio-social effects, we might call the infra-social determinants of the built environment. If Architecture ignores these factors, architects fail to rethink the role of architecture in serving society and thus engage in structural violence.

Although it can often be valuable, an appropriate proximal intervention does not entail providing free services to poor clients. Instead, architects must demystify the infra-social dialogue between clients and architecture. Empowerment acts against "structural violence" and an architect's training latently provides him the tools to empower. We do a great disservice to our profession and the built environment to ignore this.

The most direct way to combat the violence of architecture is to resist what the limited frame

so easily allows: a space where the a-political is possible. When architects pretend to work outside of politics, they engage in a form of architecture that only reinforces the structures of power that are required to purchase architecture in the first place. When an architecture of privilege is deployed, when our celebrated buildings are only corporate headquarters, private residences, and art museums, and when the best architectural minds are not engaged to assist the most disenfranchised, architecture fails to define its relevance as an art form and as a discipline. Structural violence ensues, at its worst joined by physical violence, and the Whole of Architecture is made impossible.

1. Farmer PE, Nizeye B, Stulac S, Keshavjee S, 2006 "Structural Violence and Clinical Medicine." PLoS Med 3(10): e449 doi: 10.137/journal.pmed.0030449

2. Celik, Zeynep. "Cultural Intersections: Re-visioning Architecture and the city in the Twentieth Century." At the end of the century: one hundred years of architecture : [exhibition, Los Angeles, Museum of contemporary art]. Los Angeles: The Museum of Contemporary Art ;, 1998. 192-228.

3. Farmer, 2006.

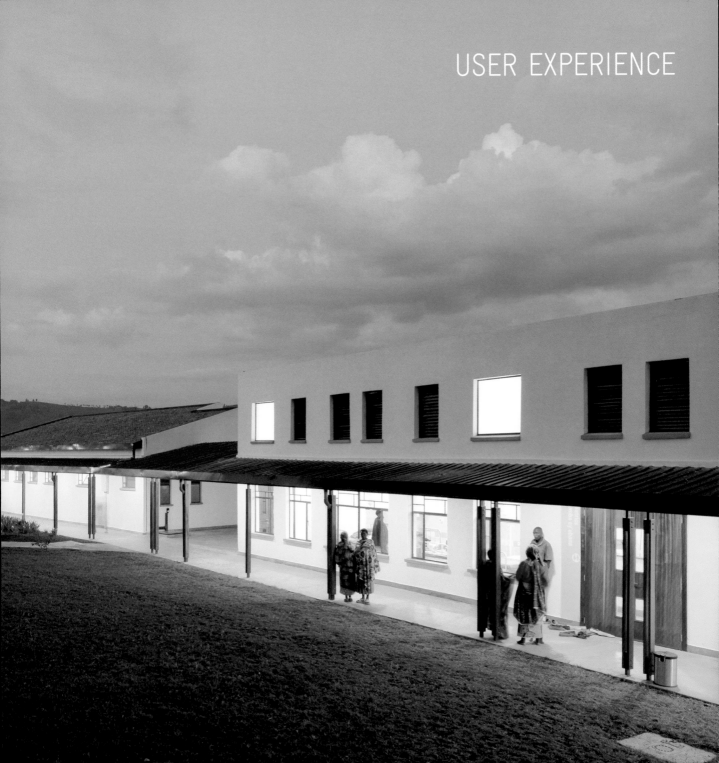

USER EXPERIENCE

STRATEGY 1
PATIENT-CENTRIC DESIGN

Patient View

In a typical hospital ward, patient beds line the perimeter of an open room. Calibrated for efficient use of space and speed of medical professionals doing rounds, beds cram against walls and the center is left free for circulation. While this is efficient and logical, <u>we were struck by the patient's experience of lying in a bed, looking at a room full of other sick patients</u>. With such a beautiful countryside and landscape in Rwanda, we decided to invert this layout and give each patient a view of a window as well as a greater sense of privacy.

While isolation in individual rooms would be ideal for infection control, often this option is not available in resource poor settings due to increased staffing needs, which can be problematic if patients are then overlooked. By using a half-height wall down the center of the ward, patient privacy is increased while allowing for supervision from a central point. Additionally, this panelized wall creates flexibility for bringing services, like electricity and oxygen, to the patient beds.

This simple design strategy provides other opportunities for a better patient experience and healthier facility. Removing beds from the perimeter allows for a larger window size, increases the opportunity for natural ventilation, a key component of the infection control strategy, and increases the amount of natural light.

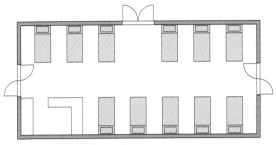

Typical general ward.

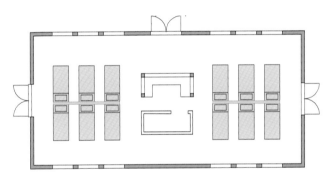

General ward redesigned for improved patient view.

Place Making

The conduit wall played an additional role as a marker of place and identity through the use of vibrant color. By focusing only on the services provided, many wards and hospital spaces fail to consider the experience and environment from the patient's perspective. Simple moves such as strategic use of bright color and designing from the patient's point of view not only provide variation and delight, but allow for a sense of place making.

At Butaro, each ward was assigned a color to introduce variation and legibility to the campus. Additionally, this provided an alternative wayfinding system for patients unable to read the signage. In our scheme, orange denotes the women's ward, yellow is pediatrics, and deep blue colors the men's ward. Turquoise is the post-operative ward, emergency is green, purple is delivery, and administration is signaled with white.

Place making, of course, is not only a localized effort. The Butaro Hospital is the first of its kind in the entire district of Burera, and locating it in a very remote region - the town of Butaro - will bring investment, economic growth, and national attention to this previously overlooked community. To not prioritize the architectural implications of this new center would be to neglect the responsibility we have to the population of Butaro who are leveraging this project to create a new identity for the village around both top medical service and as a national model of development.

STRATEGY 2
ENVIRONMENTAL APPROACH

Landscape Design

The landscape plays a critical role in rainwater management, infection control, wayfinding through the facility, and the creation of dignified environments for treatment. Landscape design ties an appropriate environmental strategy to health outcomes through infection control as well as an approach to sustainability.

Well-planned exterior environments throughout a facility's campus can provide patients a greater sense of privacy, cool air entering patient rooms, and help drain rainfall away from the building. Increased vegetation and patient views to gardens have also been shown to reduce stress and pain perception, as well as retain nurses within health care facilities.

In the Butaro Hospital, we planted trees and shrubs to help stabilize a steep hillside. Additionally, we created shaded seating areas throughout the campus that encourage patients to remain outside where the chance of airborne disease transmission is greatly reduced. In the same spirit, a children's play area was placed in the central courtyard. We also minimized hardscaped areas, favoring semipermeable landscaping to prevent the formation of pools of water, which can serve as breeding sites for vector-borne diseases. With well-designed pathways, improved wayfinding and a deliberate circulation strategy, landscaping is instrumental in improving health outcomes.

Wayfinding

A clear wayfinding system in a hospital represents a transparent and approachable administrative structure. <u>The more nebulous and difficult the circulation of a medical facility is, the more likely the patient's medical experience is to be frustrating and even ineffective.</u> The design of the signage system becomes an opportunity for guidance, as well as improved care, by making visible the pathways to available services.

In developing the circulation through the facility, we were careful to consider not only the question of navigation, but also contextually relevant issues such as gender appropriate separation, systems to assist illiterate patients, facilities for religious worship, space for accompanying family caregivers, and access by physically handicapped patients.

Designed by Vignelli Associates, the bilingual signage was color coded and made contextually appropriate to improve the experience of patients of all levels of literacy and mobility as well as encourage appropriate distribution of patients throughout the campus, further reducing the likelihood of disease transmission.

Outdoor Areas

We treated open air waiting areas and spaces for socializing as opportunities to not only enhance the patient's experience at the hospital but also to improve the quality of care and control the spread of infection.

This strategy was also a response to the local context. As is common in Rwanda, patients are often accompanied by family members who wash clothing and assist with food preparation. In the exterior plan, we wove together seating areas with stunning views and areas for cooking food and washing clothes. Visitors and patients thus benefit from contextually necessary amenities and therapeutic outdoor waiting areas.

Additionally, by removing potentially large and densely confined groups of people from interior spaces, the spread and transmission of communicable diseases can be reduced. In climates where it is feasible, being outside has also been shown to have several positive effects on a broad range of health outcomes, not limited to infectious disease.

Eliminating indoor corridors and waiting spaces is also cost effective as it reduces the square footage and makes better use of planned space. This allows for more patient beds and increased space per patient.

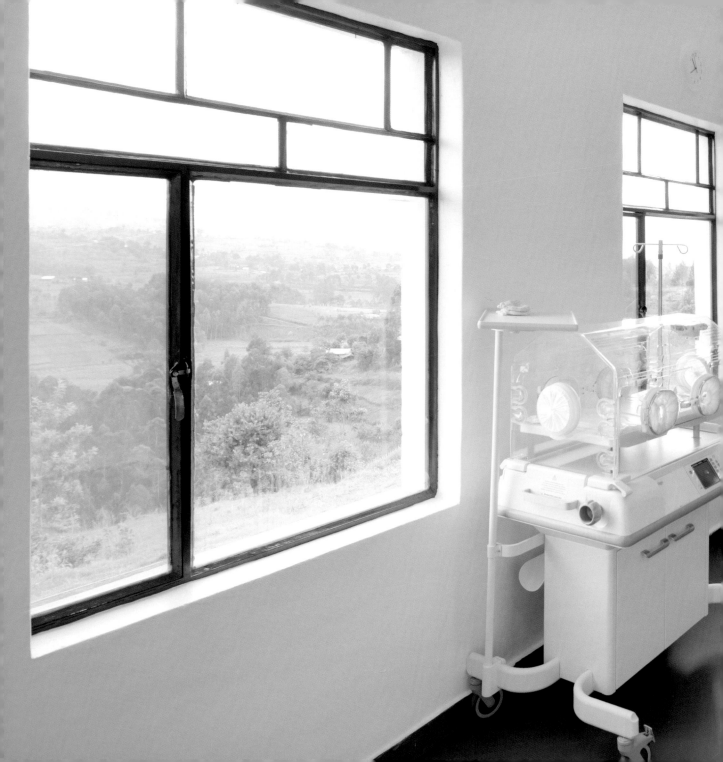

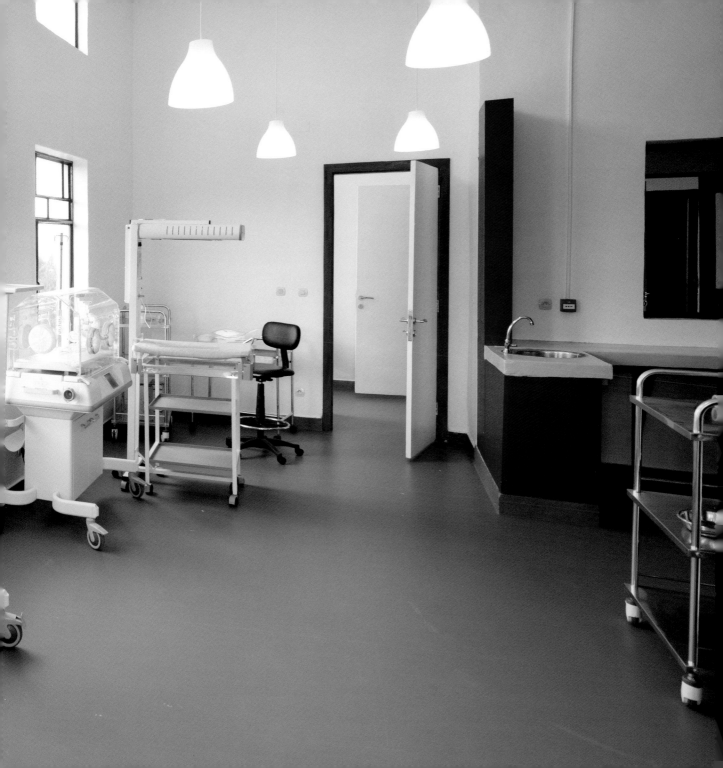

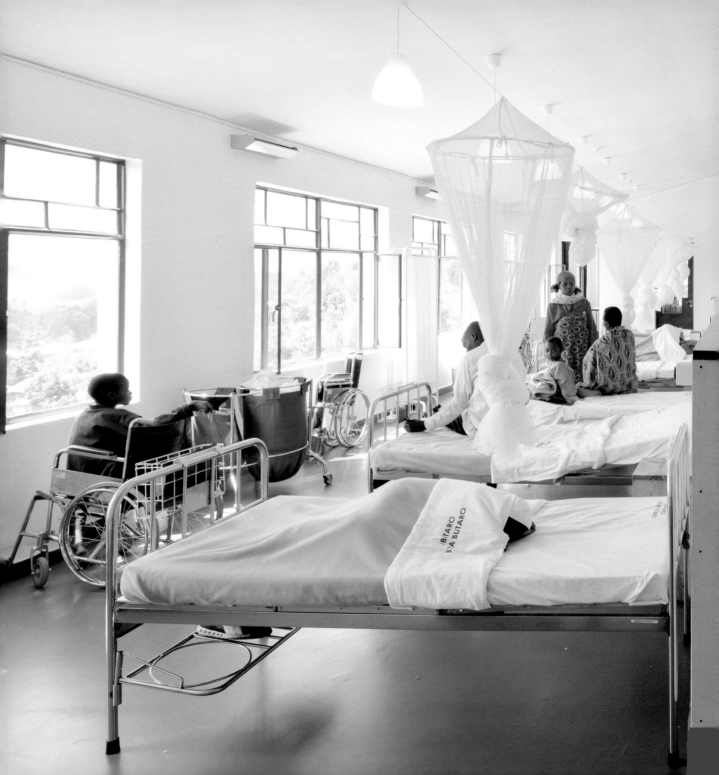

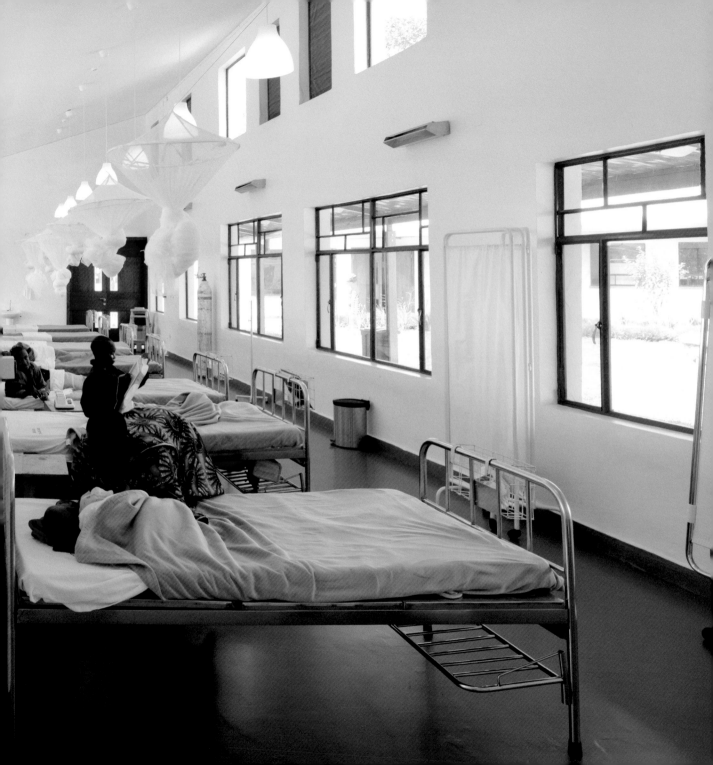

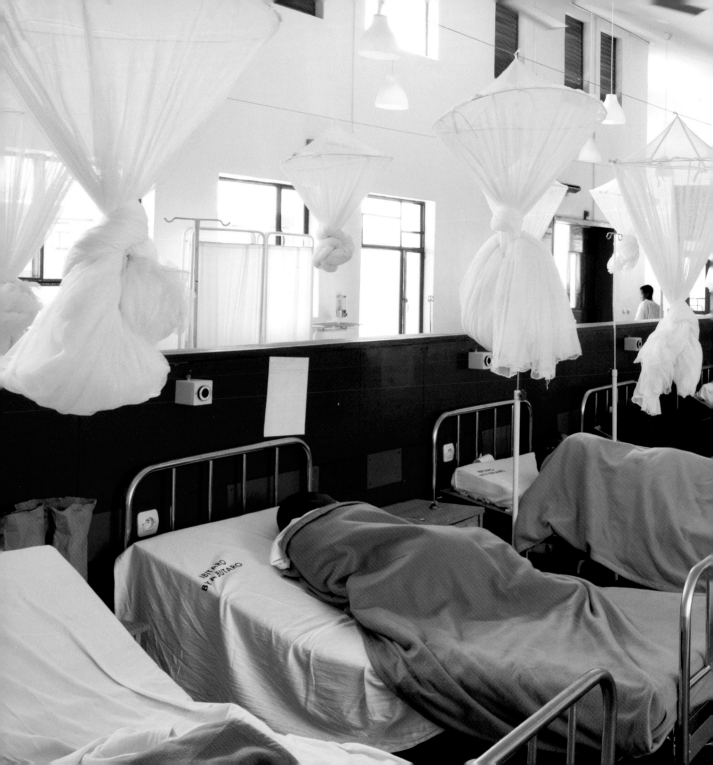

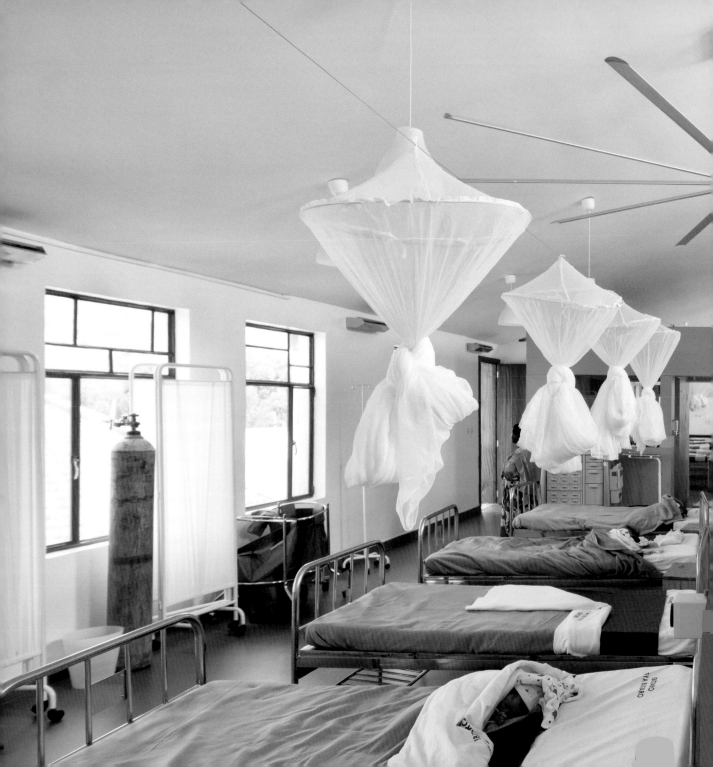

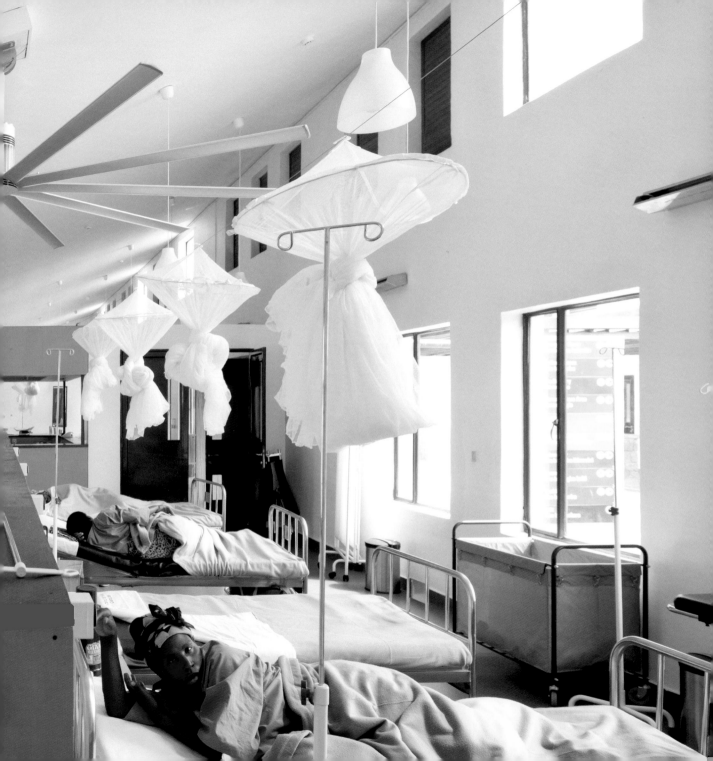

COORDINATING THE USER EXPERIENCE

First-Class Care in Rwanda
Patients at Butaro Hospital have access to a full array of medical facilities including an operating theater, mental health clinic, and this intensive care unit. More than any other group, the poorest patients truly need the highest quality facilities.

Integrated Services
Located adjacent to the operating rooms and ICU, the post-operative ward was conceived to improve the quality of care and facilitate the healing process through a sanitary, isolated design.

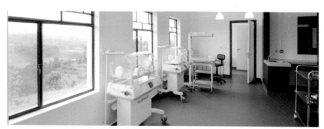

Creating a Precedent
The dedicated maternity unit comprises pre-delivery and delivery wards as well as Rwanda's first rural NICU (neonatal intensive care unit). This both meets the needs of the local population and sets the standard for any new health facility.

Patient-centered Wards
Wards in Butaro were designed to give the patients the best possible hospital visit. Orienting the beds outward from the center conduit wall means that patients look out onto healing views and receive maximum amounts of sunlight and fresh air.

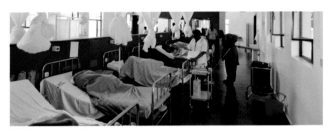

Efficient use of Space

Utilization of general wards and the separation of men's (blue), women's (orange) and pediatric (yellow) units allow the maximum number of patients to receive care without compromising their comfort.

Healing Environments

Restricting the facility to a one-room wide layout ensures that each room has at least two fenestrated walls. This promotes natural lighting and cross-ventilation while giving each patient a view of the surrounding mountains or landscaped courtyard.

Respite

All interior spaces at Butaro are oriented towards and connected to the surrounding environment, often including patio areas where patients can sit, creating a calming effect in the wards and promoting faster recovery.

STRATEGY 3
APPROPRIATE TECHNOLOGY

Local Assets

Appropriate design uses as many locally available resources as possible in order to provide contextually relevant solutions to pressing problems. This notion seems obvious when considering materials, but the importation of expertise and technology is also problematic, creating technocratic control and dependency that can lead to exploitative systems.

The notion of contextual response is a holistic concept based on local sensitivity. The goal is to create an appropriate approach and a resulting project that addresses inherently localized needs. In medical facilities, which often depend on advanced diagnostic technology, this method of contextual response includes training people to use new technology, as well as budgeting to maintain it. The same applies to architecture and infrastructure, where local materials should be prioritized, and advanced technology used only when the expertise and budget are available to maintain them.

When choosing doors, windows and furniture for Butaro, we eschewed when possible factory-produced items that would have to be imported at a high cost and with no additional benefit to the local community. Instead, we invested in training local workers in woodworking. The custom finishings at the hospital are thus both a point of pride and a source of jobs.

Understanding the resources and demographics of the population for whom the facility is being planned is a key strategy in determining which technologies, services, and design interventions should take place. The result is not only an investment in existing local material and human capital, but an approach which confronts technocratic control, an effect which can destabilize communities and local economies for generations to come.

Stack

Venturi

Chimney

Cross

Windcatcher

Ventilation

Most modern hospitals use mechanical ventilation systems to increase Air Changes per Hour (ACH) in an effort to control airborne infections. In resource-limited settings, however, these systems are often not locally available, difficult to maintain, and expensive to operate. Natural ventilation, if well designed, can be an adequate alternative. Due to the minimal maintenance and reduced operational costs, natural (or passive) systems are more appropriate in such contexts, climate permitting.

In Butaro, we used a combination of natural ventilation and low-maintenance mechanical units such as ceiling and exhaust fans to create an effective mixed-mode system.

There are many passive strategies that can be used depending upon the climate and contextual conditions. Stack effect utilizes a temperature and pressure differential to create a natural flow of air through a building. Rising hot air exhausts through the clerestory vents, creating a suction that pulls in cooler air below. A solar chimney and the Venturi effect can accelerate the stack effect, creating pockets of hot air trapped in upper chambers and pulling air through the longest sections of the building. Wind catchers, sometimes used in dense urban conditions, especially in desert climates, bring air into a building by driving flow through a system on the roof.

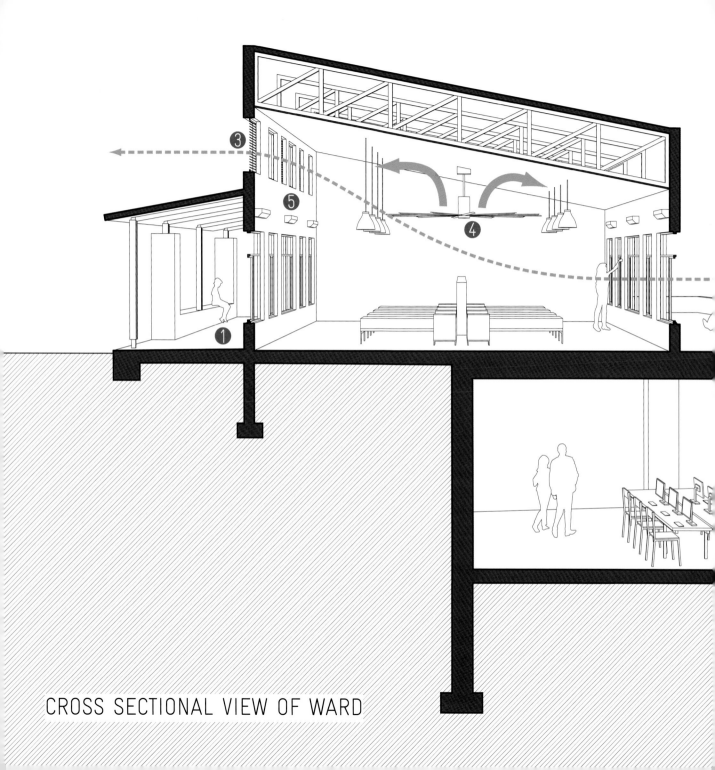

CROSS SECTIONAL VIEW OF WARD

1. Exterior Circulation
2. Cross Ventilation
3. Inoperable Vents
4. Industrial Fans
5. Ultraviolet Germicidal Lights

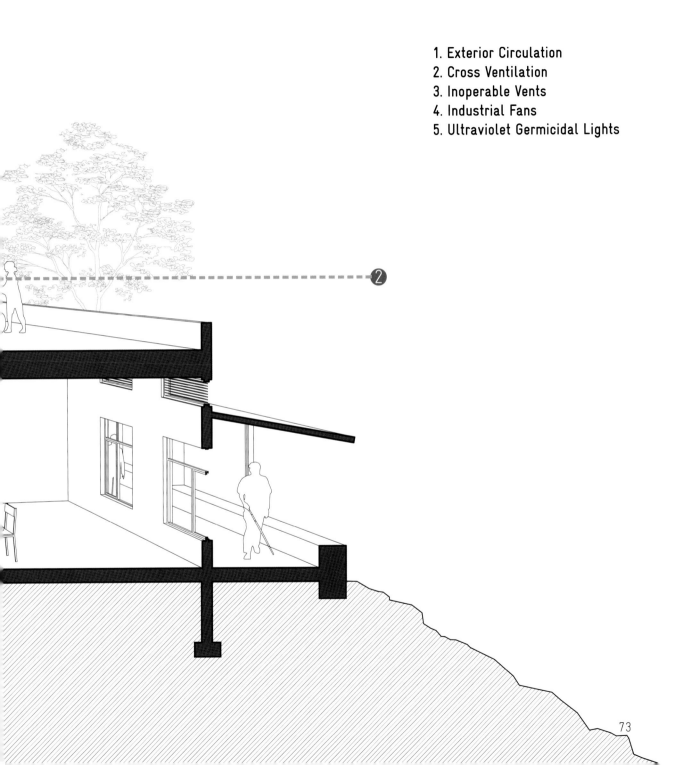

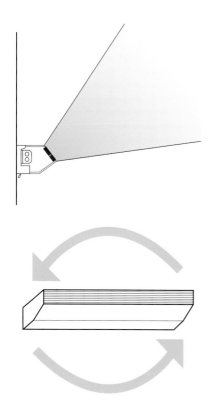

UVGI fixtures often include shields or louvers, which orient them upwards and prevent them from being in the direct line of sight.

UVGI Lights

Ultraviolet Germicidal Irradiation (UVGI) fixtures use a bulb that emits light at wavelengths which deactivate many diseases carried in microscopic airborne droplets. We placed UVGI lights in all of the wards at the Butaro Hospital in order to further lower the risk of infection and disease transmission. Since UVGI is most effective in the upper part of the room, we designed wards to generate an air mixing effect that circulates contaminated air into this zone. The fixtures with exposed UVGI light were placed 3m above the floor, outside of direct eye contact to avoid temporary eye irritation caused by this light.

Microscopic droplets are a hazard because they transmit diseases such as TB when infected people cough. In a hospital setting, this intermingling of germs can lead to drug resistance and the emergence of more virulent and dangerous strains of a disease. UVGI mitigates this problem and can be installed throughout buildings where a significant risk of airborne infection has been identified. The UVGI lights help to stimulate air exchange by 'cleansing' existing air that can be recirculated free of diseases.

While UVGI lights are one effective strategy to confront airborne disease, they are not the only strategy and work best in tandem with other mixed-mode systems. However, as a more advanced technology, UVGI lights require proper training and maintenance.

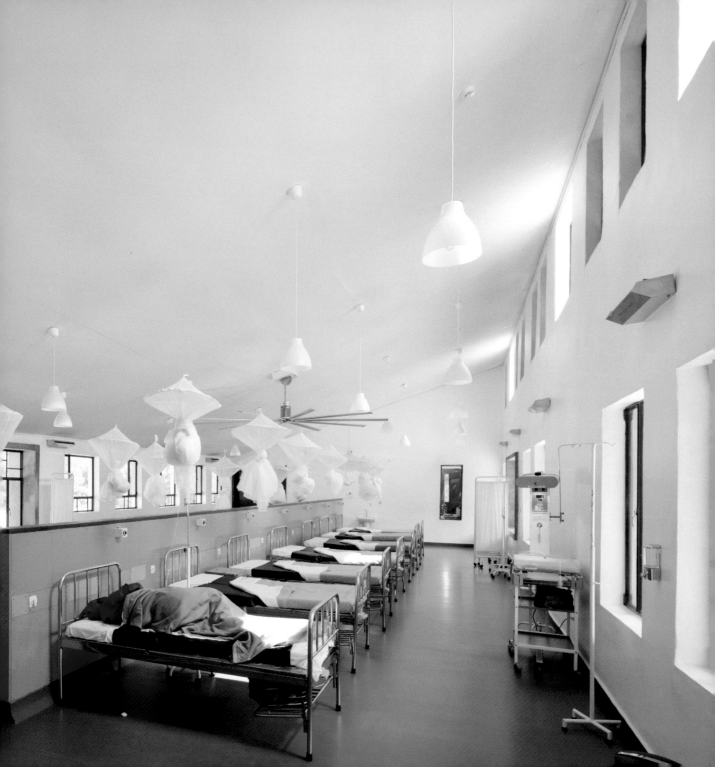

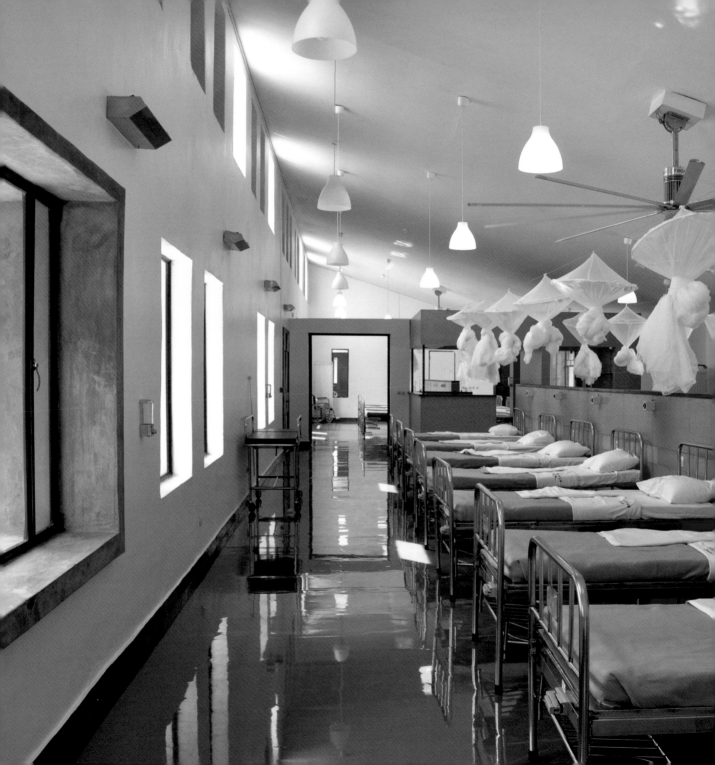

Low Maintenance Resiliency

We made use of industrial scale fans to generate large amounts of air mixing in the wards. With a diameter of four meters, the fans provide a high volume airflow over a large area. The benefit of this system is two-fold: Not only is air circulation increased throughout the open space, but it moves at a slower velocity. This results in less draft directly over the patients, keeping body temperature relatively constant. To our knowledge, this is the first use of these fans in a medical setting.

In addition, we configured the fans to rotate so that air is pulled into the upper part of the room instead of pushed downwards. This effect creates an environment of consistent mixing, bringing air to be treated or exhausted in the upper part of the room, while keeping patients comfortable.

Through the combination of UVGI lights deactivating germs in the air, stack ventilation drawing air through the room, and large fans mixing air within the space, we created a series of complementary systems that operate to increase airflow and decrease infection rates. All of this is accomplished with very little energy input and limited maintenance.

By specifying complementary systems that are each simple and effective, a powerful, resilient structure is formed. All of these systems are effective; thus if any of the three parts fail, the other two will continue to circulate and cleanse the air.

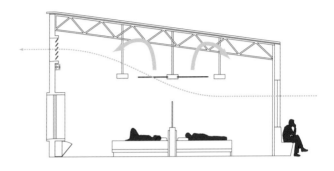

With the help of upwards facing, large-radius fans, air passing through the ward is pulled into the upper areas of the ward, where it is either deactivated by UVGI lighting or exhausted through clerestory vents.

STRATEGY FOUR
MASTER PLAN AND SITING

Strategic Siting

Choosing the most appropriate location can greatly impact a health facility. Some of the most significant problems that occur with health facilities over time are due to inadequate planning for growth and evolution. Often, buildings and services are added to the core facility that compromise the functionality of the original design.

The appropriate site has symbolic and economic implications as well. For the Butaro Hospital, our partners chose the most strategic hilltop in the Burera region in order to maximize views and airflow. The hilltop was previously occupied by a Rwandan Military camp. They agreed to relocate for the hospital to be built, acknowledging its symbolic value for Rwanda's shift towards investment in human capital, health, and education.

Furthermore, the hospital is bringing dynamic economic development to the region. Originally located in a remote village without electricity, the project has brought growth and services that are improving the lives of the people in Burera.

CAMPUS MASSING STUDY

Multistory

Multistory facilities are good in urban settings where space is limited for building. It is important to ensure that backup generators are reliable in the case of an outage so that lifts can continue to operate. If not, planners should consider large scale ramp systems that are able to reach upper floors.

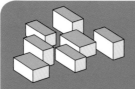

Campus

Breaking the departments into small, separate buildings is recommended for isolating different diseases and infection control. The plan allows for breezes to flow through the campus, and increases the options for windows and direction of air circulation in each ward. It also provides more surface area for rainwater catchment and/or solar panel installation.

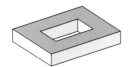

Courtyard

Courtyard schemes provide a protected outdoor space where patients and visitors can be easily observed. Weather permitting, workers can utilize paths in the center to efficiently access the different wards, and the layout allows for decentralized nursing stations throughout the building.

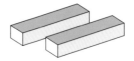

Bar

A bar plan is beneficial for a rural setting that provides fewer specialties and services to its targeted population. This plan utilizes one story for greater handicap accessibility and provides increased surface area for solar panel installment and/or rain water catchment.

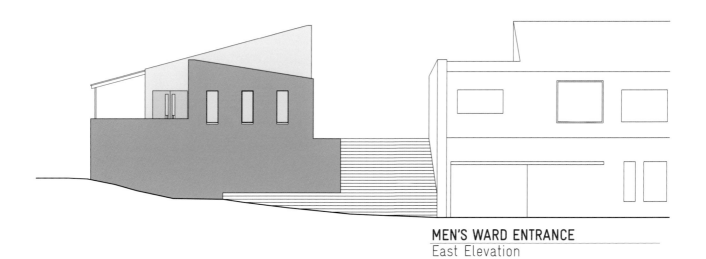

MEN'S WARD ENTRANCE
East Elevation

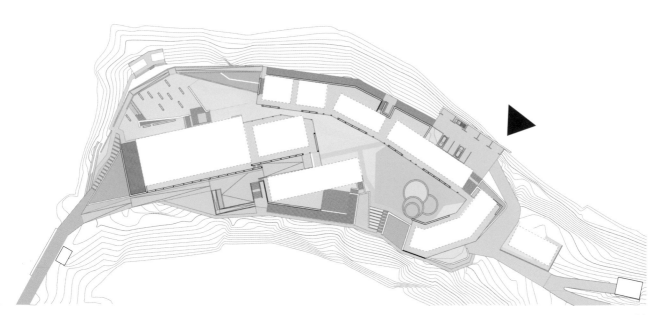

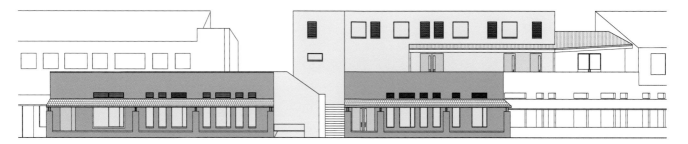

LL. ADMINISTRATIVE BLOCK / UL. MATERNITY
East Elevation

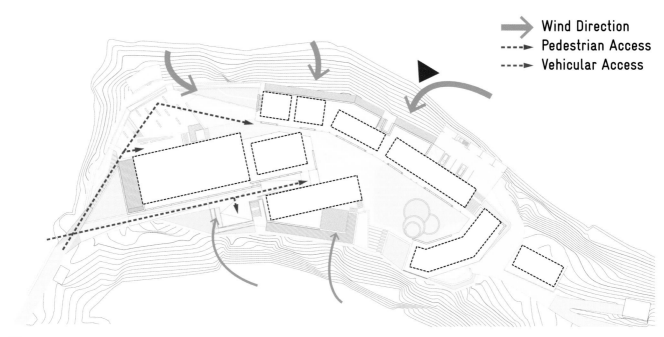

→ Wind Direction
----▶ Pedestrian Access
----▶ Vehicular Access

Program Arrangement

The configuration of the buildings can vary widely to accommodate programmatic, contextual, and climatic needs. The massing can help in infection control as well by calibrating the pedestrian circulation between departments and minimizing overlap with potentially infectious patients.

With strong prevailing winds, the buildings in Butaro were placed in a manner that takes advantage of those air currents for natural ventilation. Additionally, we strategically broke and staggered the building units to allow for natural wind patterns to cut down on the energy needs and cost of the mechanical systems.

The goal for Butaro, being in a resource-constrained setting, was to develop a flexible campus that uniquely responded to the particular context of rural Rwanda. Instead of a hospital based on standards developed outside of Rwanda, the Butaro design sought to improve upon international standards by configuring its buildings to be most appropriate for the needs of the community and the context of the site.

When drawing up a master plan and choosing a site for a health facility, vehicular and patient access, access to reliable sources of water, and the slope of the site for erosion and drainage must also be taken into consideration.

Guidance and Circulation

Navigating the facility is not only important for efficiency of work flow, but plays a critical role in infection control and patient experience. Orchestrating the flow of patients, staff, and equipment through the hospital to minimize unnecessary overlap reduces exposure to possible infection and allows for improved distribution of people throughout the campus.

In the Butaro design, we took care to minimize exposure between immunosuppressed patients, like those with HIV, and more infectious patients like those with TB. However, it was also important to make efforts to reduce the stigmatization that can accompany isolation.

Certain areas of the facility required a more advanced focus on circulation, such as the procession through surgery. The design choreographs the flow of the patient through admission, anesthesia, surgery, and post-operative recovery, minimizing exposure to potential infections and overlap with the flow of doctors and nurses.

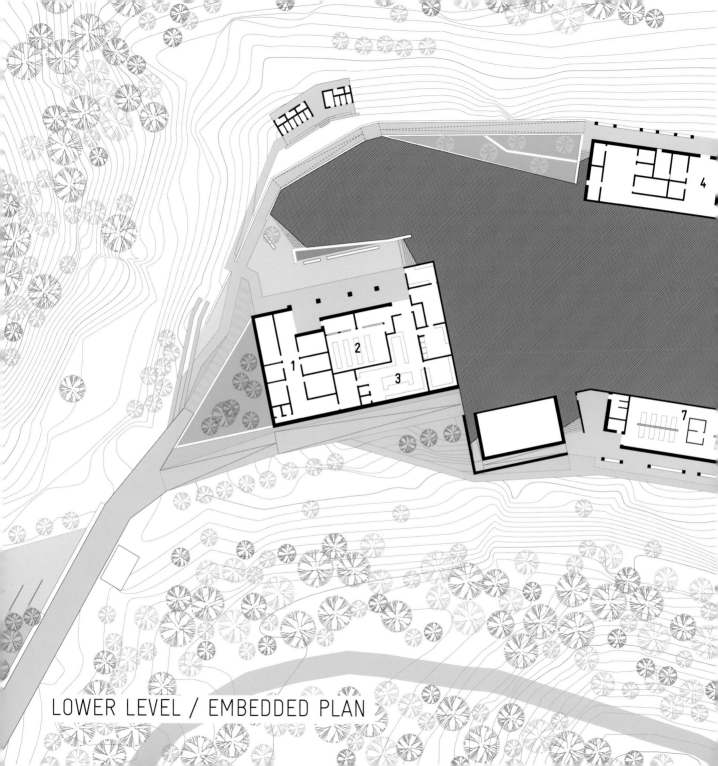

LOWER LEVEL / EMBEDDED PLAN

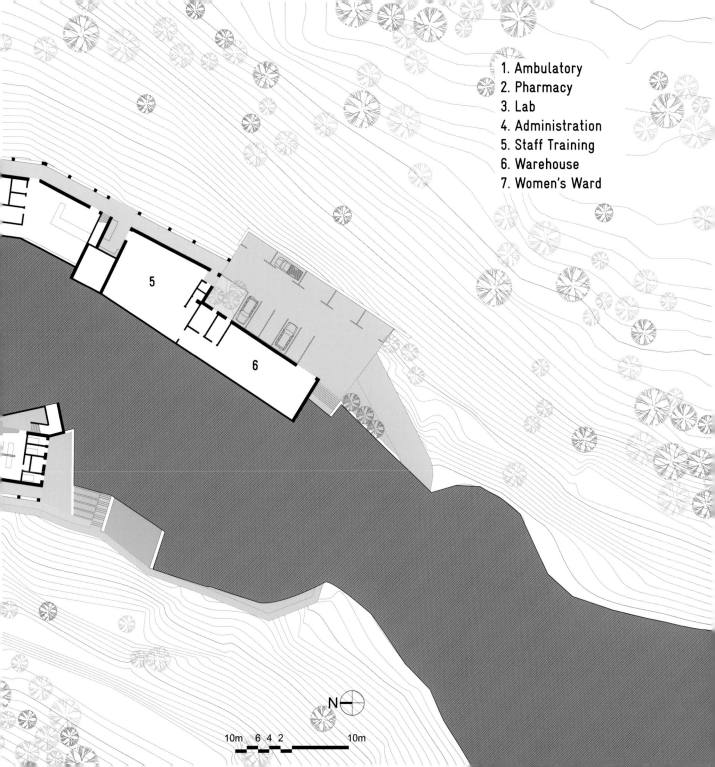

1. Ambulatory
2. Pharmacy
3. Lab
4. Administration
5. Staff Training
6. Warehouse
7. Women's Ward

5

6

N

10m 6 4 2   10m

UPPER LEVEL / COURTYARD PLAN

1. Intensive Care Unit
2. Post-Operative Ward
3. Operating Room
4. Emergency Room
5. Neonatal ICU
6. Delivery
7. Pre-Delivery
8. Pediatric Ward
9. Post-Partum Ward
10. Men's Ward
11. Laundry

N

10m 6 4 2   10m

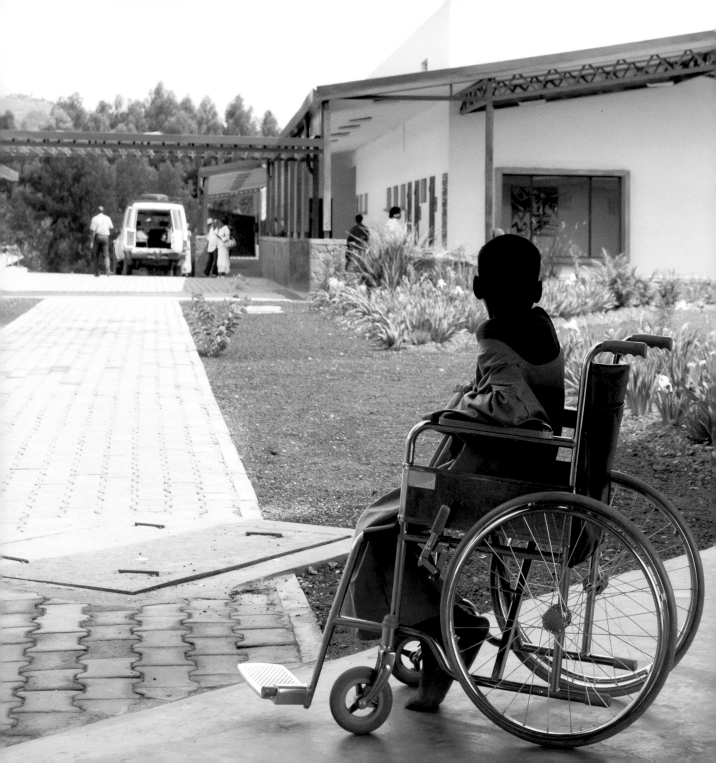

CONTEXTUALLY RESPONSIVE CAMPUS

Health Care Campus
The campus-style building layout aids in disease isolation and infection control. Refreshing breezes flow through the campus, and windows proliferate, providing fresh air to each ward.

Lower Level Plan
Outpatient, administrative, and support services are on the lower level, which is embedded in the hillside. This creates a natural division between patient and staff spaces.

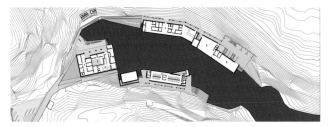

Upper Level Plan
Inpatient wards are positioned on the upper level. This permits easy access by doctors and takes advantage of the hospital's hilltop setting for cross ventilation and exterior, open-air patient circulation.

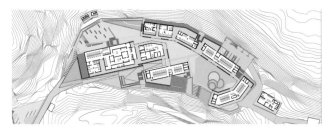

Prioritizing Pedestrians
The hospital entrance welcomes patients and visitors alike. It also serves the critical function of separating vehicular and non-motorized traffic. Since many of the patients arrive on foot, it is important to prioritize the pedestrian circulation.

Choreographing Waiting

Providing a variety of landscaped and dignified exterior spaces for incoming patients and visitors to gather reduces overcrowding in interior areas where infection is more likely to occur. Additionally, the patient and visitor experience is improved.

Functional Landscaping

Planted courtyards invite patients and visitors to be outdoors. The native vegetation increases biodiversity as well as absorbs rain, avoiding pools of water that might serve as breeding grounds for disease.

Universal Access

Conscientious programming of the campus ensures that patients of all ages and mobilities are able to access services and amenities. This is particularly important in countries like Rwanda where accommodation of disabled persons is not the norm.

Physical Context

The Butaro Hospital sits on a hilltop in Burera that was once a military base. While providing stunning views, it also acts as a symbolic beacon of healing to the rest of the district.

Outdoor Moments

The hilltop location of the hospital also opens the campus up to cooling breezes. The design furnishes many outdoor patios for gatherings or quiet reflection.

Medical Capacity

Prior to 2007, Burera District had no hospital and no physicians to service its 340,000 residents. Now there is a 140-bed hospital with 12 full-time physicians on staff. Over 1500 community health workers link outlying villages to health facilities.

Landscape Features

Butaro's mild climate provides an ideal environment for outdoor activities. Amenities such as strategically placed water features further invite patients and doctors beyond the hospital walls.

Exterior Circulation

Placing circulation on the outside of the facility has multiple positive effects: disease transmission is reduced, healing views are maximized and interior space is freed up for active treatment areas.

Design for Reduced Risk of Infection
This hospital was designed without hallways. Thus, outdoor waiting areas function to disperse crowds from poorly ventilated spaces, reducing the spread and transmission of communicable diseases.

Outdoor Pharmacy
Drug dispensaries that are accessible from outdoor circulation areas, with several consult stations, help the patients filter through in a timely fashion with less crowding.

Culturally Adapted Spaces
Cultures that typically have larger families accompanying patients to the health facility benefit from designated outdoor areas. This accommodates visitation while minimizing congestion and the risk of infection.

COMMUNITY IMPACT

STRATEGY FIVE
MEASURED OUTCOMES

Mortality & Morbidity Reduction

Just as medical professionals carefully measure the results of their work in number of lives saved and incidences of disease avoided, architects have the opportunity to measure a building's role in preventing deaths, saving lives, and improving health outcomes.

To treat the hospital as simply a meaningless shell in which medical services are provided is to ignore the way in which the facility itself must operate as a system, a medical device that over time, and through varying constraints, can have profound impacts on a population's health. <u>To consider the hospital instead as another preventive tool in the limited arsenal of global health doctors is to recognize the need to more accurately analyze the building's success and failure rates.</u> Measuring success then becomes a fundamental component, as with any technology, of evaluating the investment in a system over time and its ability to improve the health of the population served.

Post-occupancy Assessment

It is said that eighty percent of a building's costs come after it is constructed. For medical facilities, especially those funded by NGO's and outside donors, this expense must be an integral consideration from the beginning to determine the form and services available in the construction of a new building. The architect's work should not be considered completed at the ribbon cutting.

In Butaro, the improved design projects a reduction in transmission rates of nosocomial infections, an increase in patients served through an awareness of additional services, and an improvement in doctor retention through improved facilities. These projections, while likely to occur, will be studied and analyzed through randomized trials and clinical studies to understand accurately the complete effect that improved facilities can have on a communities' total health.

STRATEGY SIX
COMMUNITY ENGAGEMENT

Training

The construction process is often a missed opportunity to train, educate and empower. Using local labor can reduce construction cost, create community buy-in to the project, and leave lasting positive impact by providing the community with job skills.

New methods and technologies are emerging today that make use of readily available and low-cost resources for structurally sound building. Likewise, looking at the entire construction process to see if local labor can be utilized will turn the process of construction into an engine for economic development and stability.

Relying on local labor, as Partners In Health and MASS did in Butaro, is not simply an ethical strategy to train and build stronger local economies; it is also a strategy to resist technocratic systems that control local communities through imported technologies, expertise, and inappropriate approaches.

Craft and Economic Development

The Butaro Hospital incorporated the volcanic earth stone found in the Burera District of Rwanda. This material choice required the training of local craftsmen in the art of masonry, a skill that they were able to market throughout Rwanda after the completion of the hospital.

Partners In Health and MASS strategically integrated craft development as a way to reduce costs, but also to improve quality and create jobs while deploying locally produced, customized finishes wherever possible. Carpenters were trained on site to design and build nearly every piece of furniture, door, column, and window-frame. Masons constructed the walls, and a multitude of newly-trained laborers excavated the site by hand.

The strategy of utilizing high-intensity, local labor serves not only to return investments into the community but also to develop local craft services and optimize embedded local knowledge.

Community Input

Health facilities are important systems of civic infrastructure. If well planned, they can have far reaching and profound impacts in the community that go beyond simply providing health care. By using predominantly local materials in the construction of a health facility, planners and builders can create opportunities to improve local construction practices and empower communities of craftspeople. Additionally, this can significantly reduce construction costs by cutting down on transportation fees, while providing valuable jobs to the local community and garnering support for the project.

Community buy-in is a fundamental component to any infrastructure project in creating an appropriate planning strategy that involves local input and local impact. Conversely, the reliance on imported materials and imported labor can create systems dependent upon outside control for maintenance. This a-contextual thinking is a form of imported control often found in resource-limited settings that should be avoided at any cost.

Looked at in this way, design choices from material decisions to construction processes have far reaching impacts on the total health of communities.

BUILDING BUTARO HOSPITAL

Community-Sourced Construction
By using local labor rather than importing heavy machinery, 12,000 short-term unskilled jobs were created, distributing over $500,000 in income to the district.

Engendering Local Ownership
The use of local labor also created a sense of ownership in the community – the hospital truly belongs to Butaro and will remain a source of pride for years to come.

Leaving a Legacy
In the course of building the Butaro Hospital, MASS employees helped write the curriculum for Rwanda's first school of architecture, recognizing the potential of local architects for rebuilding the country and creating impact far beyond Burera.

Transmission of Knowledge
Many of the designers at MASS's Kigali office continue to be involved with the architecture program at the Kigali Institute of Technology where they serve as faculty members.

Adding Value
In addition to the unskilled labor used during construction, 3,898 skilled craftspeople were trained and employed.

Volcanic Stone
The locally-sourced volcanic stone makes for a unique and bold facade. The stonework was also a major point of pride for the local construction crew who developed a unique stonemasonry technique through the process.

Building Local Capacity
Creating workshops on site yielded skilled carpenters and furniture makers, limiting the need to import goods. These craftspeople now have skills to market to other projects in Rwanda and beyond.

CONCLUSION
DIGNITY CONSTRUCTION

In applying the highest standards of design and building to the poorest places and the most underserved communities, what is constructed first and foremost is dignity.

Well-built infrastructure is the crystallization of well-conceived services and successful community input. The building is the physical manifestation of this, but its process of conception and its effects after construction represent the more expansive opportunities for positive impact in the community.

The first of these effects are the services that the project helps to facilitate, either through adequate planning or innovative solutions. The second is its operation as a tool in the creation of healthier environments, practices, and communities. The final impact is an architecture that acts as a symbol of growth, identity, and dignity to a community. This is a service and aspiration that, to date, by serving mostly those who can afford it, architecture has largely been unable to provide to the majority of the world.

The Butaro Hospital is an effort to question the assumption that the poor deserve anything less than the best services, be it health care or architecture. Rather, Partners In Health teaches us that more than any group, the poor deserve the best possible services and facilities that are available.

VITAL STATISTICS

Burera District Before

Prior to 2007, one of the last districts in Rwanda without a hospital.
Population: 340,000
Physicians: 0

Burera District After

Over 1500 community health workers in every village link patients to 15 health centers, which in turn feed the new public hospital. Over 90% of the district's inhabitants now possess health insurance, and there are 12 physicians and over 300 nurses on staff in the district.

Butaro Hospital Amenities

140 new ward beds
2 operating rooms
1 emergency procedure room
Fully equipped lab
Neonatology unit, planned for 4 incubators
Post-maternity ward
Delivery ward with 4 beds
2 infant resuscitation tables
ER with 4 trauma bays
10 isolation rooms
Two digital X-ray systems
The district's first comprehensive mental health
   clinic and inpatient facility

The Butaro Hospital runs on 100% hydro-electric power from a newly constructed dam located one mile from the facility in Rusumo.

Fluid dynamics experts predict an air-change rate that will exceed 12 air changes per hour in wards. This improvement is anticipated to reduce nosocomial transmissions by 35% as has been seen in comparable cases.

Built Area: 6,040 square meters
Cost: $4.4M
Design Phase: January 2008 – December 2009
Construction Phase: February 2009-January 2011

ACKNOWLEDGEMENTS

Partners: Government of Rwanda, Rwandan Ministry of Health, Partners In Health / Inshuti Mu Buzima, Clinton Health Access Initiative, MASS Design Group

Architectural Design Team
Michael Murphy, Alan Ricks, Sierra Bainbridge, Marika Clark, Ryan Leidner, Garret Gantner, Cody Birkey, Ebbe Strathairn, Maura Rockcastle, Dave Saladik, Alda Ly, Robert Harris, Commode Dushimimana, Nicolas Rutikanga

Landscape Design: Sierra Bainbridge and Maura Rockcastle

Structural Engineering: ICON

Construction Supervision: PIH/IMB, Bruce Nizeye, Felix Ndagijimana

Sewage Plant Engineering: EcoProtection

Signage Design: Vignelli Associates

Book Design Team: Michael Murphy, Alan Ricks, Elizabeth Timme, Kyle Williams, Monique Guimond, Tanya Paz

Photos: Photos by Iwan Baan except pages: *2, 4, 8, 10, 22, 26, 32, 44, 49, 48, 62, 66, 68, 76, 84, 85, 95, 100, 120, 123, 126, 127, 129, 130, 131, 132, 134, 136, 138, 140, 142, 144, 151, 154, 160, 170*

Sappi Design That Matters

The publication of this book was made possible by a Sappi *Ideas That Matter* grant. In 1999, Sappi Fine Paper North America established the *Ideas that Matter* program to recognize and support designers who generously donate their time and talent to a wide range of charitable activities. Even today, *Ideas that Matter* remains the only grant program of its kind in the industry. Since its creation, *Ideas that Matter* has contributed $11 million worldwide to causes that enhance our lives, our communities and our planet. Sappi shares with MASS the belief that design is about much more than the object and can be a powerful force for positive change. MASS thanks Sappi for the opportunity to make this book a reality and share our story with the world.

Iwan Baan

Despite only taking up architectural photography in 2005, Iwan Baan has become the preeminent architecture photographer of our day. Coming from the Netherlands, he recently won the inaugural Julius Shulman Institute Photography Award and has been featured extensively in hundreds of publications and profiled in The New York Times. Like MASS, Iwan has a passion for African architecture. His images elegantly capture the vibrancy and richness of Butaro, bringing the experience of walking through the hospital to those far from Rwanda. MASS is deeply indebted to Iwan for his unsurpassed artistry and generosity.

Gratitude

The Butaro Hospital, while a design story that we hope is a model for improved facilities, would not have been possible without the innovative minds that inhabit the Ministry of Health of Rwanda, the community of Butaro, Partners In Health (PIH) / Inshuti Mu Buzima (IMB), The Nova Family and our friends, mentors, accompagnateurs and supporters.

Our deepest gratitude is held for our friends at IMB, especially Dr. Peter Drobac, Dr. Michael Rich, Dr. Tharcisse Kampunga, Dr. Matt Craven, Bruce Nizeye, Felix Ndagijimana, Anne Sosin, Emmanuel Kamanzi, Jean D'Amour Kubwimana, Victor Nkurikiyinka, Elisephan Ntakirutimana, Jean Luc Mpamije, Ian Mountjoy, and all the countless others who made this possible.

Our thanks to our hosts in the Government of Rwanda, particularly His Excellency President of the Republic of Rwanda Paul Kagame, Minister of Health Dr. Agnes Binagwaho, Governor of the Northern Province Mr. Aime Bosenibamwe, Burera District Mayor Mr. Samuel Sembagare and all our friends who were instrumental in making this a reality.

We would not have been able to deliver this project without our sponsors and supporters in Kigali, especially Robert Bayigamba, who has generously hosted us in Nyarugenge and supported our work since 2009. We also rely upon the input and inspiration of our colleagues and students of the Department of Architecture and the Faculty of Architecture and Environmental Design at the Kigali Institute of Science and Technology, especially Vice Rector of Academics, John Mshana.

At Partners In Health in Boston, our thanks to Ted Constan, Ophelia Dahl and our friend Dr. Paul Farmer for believing in us.

As well, our thanks to all our supporters, mentors, and friends including Karen and Brian Conway, Rob and Emily Dyson, Jody Adams, Hashim Sarkis, and the countless others at the Graduate School of Design that supported this venture.

EMPOWERING ARCHITECTURE

Butaro Hospital, Rwanda